Fish Streets before Dawn

Also by Rick Campbell

POETRY
Provenance
Gunshot, Peacock, Dog
The History of Steel
Dixmont
Setting the World in Order
The Traveler's Companion
A Day's Work

NONFICTION
Sometimes the Light (essays)

FISH STREETS BEFORE DAWN

Poems

Rick Campbell

Press 53
Winston-Salem

Press 53, LLC
PO Box 30314
Winston-Salem, NC 27130

First Edition

Copyright © 2024 by Rick Campbell

All rights reserved, including the right of reproduction in whole or in part in any form except in the case of brief quotations embodied in critical articles or reviews. For permission, contact publisher at editor@press53.com or at the address above.

Cover photo by Rick Campbell

Author photo by Rick Campbell

Cover design by Kevin Morgan Watson

Library of Congress Control Number
2023951726

ISBN 978-1-950413-74-4

for DJL
&
Jasper

ACKNOWLEDGMENTS

The author thanks the editors of the publications where these poems first appeared, occasionally in different form:

Alabama Literary Review, "Don't Burn Again for Nothing," "Love Is Not a Victory March," "On Dying Too Soon after Finally Finding Love," "Poem for the Day John Prine Died" & "The Old Places"

Book of Matches, "Wild Lament of Saint Teresa"

Cave Wall, "In Late Recognition of Prince"

Kestrel, "Another Story of Ash," "Touching the Heart Means a Steal of Home"

Prime Number Magazine, "The Angel of Winter Won't Remember Your Name"

Sandhills Review, "Big Sur, December"

Scoundrel Time, "No Fences and an Axe"

South Florida Poetry Review, "John Prine's Band"

Susurrus, "Thinking of Frost and the Calabrian Miners Dead in West Virginia"

Contents

Introduction by Frank X. Gaspar   xi

Alligator Point

The Wild Lament of Saint Teresa   3
On the Porch with the Waxing Moon   4
New Years and the Fishmongers of London   5
No Fences and an Axe   6
Names of Water   7
Wish You Were Here   8
Tropical Storm Eta, Alligator Point   9
Requiem for a Junked Mullet Smoker   10
Just Past Dawn We Walk to the Beach   11
Throwing Starfish Back into the Sea   12
Hard Rain   13
Walking Meditation   14
The Light We Call Winter   15
Fish Streets before Dawn   16
Two Lane Highway to Panacea   17

Other Places

Touching the Heart Means a Steal of Home   21
Pittsburgh Ritual   22
Another Story of Ash   23
In Late Recognition of Prince   24
Thinking of Frost and the Calabrian Miners Dead
    in West Virginia   25
The Old Places   26
What I Might Know about Indiana   27
This Train Is Not Going to NY   28
On Each Bead We Said Three Hail Marys   29
With James Wright as My Spiritual Guide, I Drive through
    Southeast Ohio Looking for Ancestors   30
Sometimes the Song Tells You Who You Are   31
Xenoglossy   32
Derecho   33
December, Big Sur   34
Telluride, Abandoned Mine Shaft   35
Wyoming Ranch Road   36
Tucumcari   37
Practicing Silence   38

What's Been Lost

Love Is Not a Victory March	41
On Dying Too Soon after Finally Finding Love	42
Don't Burn Again for Nothing	43
Shoes and Shirts Last Longer than a Man	44
The Angel of Winter Won't Remember Your Name	45
The Rapture Coming	46
Eden	47
Pawning His Guitar	48
What's Emptiness Got to Do with It?	49
John Prine's Band	50
Instant Replay	51
Jumping the VW Bus	52
Figurative Language	53
Poem for the Day John Prine Died	54
Hide & Seek	55
Five Miles from Wherever I Am	56
Unfriending the Writer More Famous Than I	57
The Gun	58
Dream of Nowhere Home	59
About the Author	61

INTRODUCTION

I have known and enjoyed Rick Campbell's work for years, and that familiarity with his poems leads me into this new book with all my senses ready for a good read. He doesn't disappoint. *Fish Streets before Dawn* brings us all the fabric of Campbell's created worlds, and then he takes us further as his energy expands and contracts along newer avenues of thought and feeling. Campbell is one of his generation that took to America's roads and byways, old cars, hitchhiking, The Greyhound, and just plain walking. I found myself thinking of Du Fu, the troubadours of the thirteenth century and, of course, Kerouac and the Dharma Bums, but then there was more, and the more is Rick Campbell and his resolute authenticity.

He is an inspired traveler (having traveled with him a bit, I can attest to this). A partial list: Singer Island, Elwood, Manhattan, Salineville, Okeechobee Bay, Cedar Rapids, Big Sur, Telluride, Medicine Bow, Barstow, Tucumcari, and on—you get the picture. But Rick's peregrine disposition provokes more than mere touring. He is constantly thinking, meditating, looking for answers in this sector of his life's arc. Any compendium of Campbell's habits of mind, in any order, show his stance and countenance in the face of a broken world, where our attentions are pulled and pushed by its debilitating trivialities and its unspeakable horrors alike. Hear a few outcries from various poems: "Years of jerry-rigged schemes / collapsed in fire and rust."; "What's the word for walking / on water and naming it home?"; "Morning grass, still wet and cold, gleaming / like tongues of a thousand little gods."; "Four days cross country, good rides. / No one killed me."; "I'm tired. The heart's a wheel, bent / but carrying me down the road."

In the poem "Throwing Starfish Back into the Sea" he wonders how much "good he has done" with his uncertain act of kindness. It is an apt poem, and taken in the context of this collection and its outcries, we see that Rick Campbell's wanderings and questing are testimony to the core of his art: surviving, yes, but surviving as the step that allows us to pursue any small good we can bring along with us.

Frank X. Gaspar

Alligator Point

The Wild Lament of Saint Teresa

Two days' storm, the beach wrack:
grass, dark feathers from a tern,
skimmer, a gull. We talk about love
and death, suspect choices, derelict
results. We walk beyond my usual end,
and finally find it, wrapped in grass,
and shells. Its long neck curved,
not as in flight, not as in swimming,
but as in dead. I nudge its white
collar with a bare toe and think of Eberhart's
groundhog in the golden fields,
his wasp and the breath of life,
Stafford's deer tumbling over the cliff.
Here it is, a loon. We turn back
into wind slinging a rain shroud
        like a slow, soft parade.

On the Porch with the Waxing Moon

The longboarders are old now.
They sit on the porch, watch
the shore break, talk about
the sunset, the young family walking
with their flashlights, the illegal
seine netters out late last night.
It's the pandemic, yes, but it's what
their lives have wound down to
here on the edge of the land. Dog
Island's few lights glimmer and sway.
A shrimper runs toward Shell Point.
Tonight, most nights, they don't
even mention the guitars, but tell
slow stories about the lost
and far away. The kids on the beach
don't know about ghost
crabs and the moon.

New Years and the Fishmongers of London

The last mullet smoked this year
is the last my rusted smoker will give.
Years of jerry-rigged schemes
collapsed in fire and rust.

Edward the First chartered fishmongers, ancestors
of the longhaired guy in the Gators' cap
who asks how I'm doing as he wraps my purchase.
I wonder if he knows his Guild once
sponsored forty thousand mounted knights.
He has no monopoly here for crying
fish. Tractor Supply sells smokers
for less than a hundred bucks.
Sixteen mullet at his current price.

Let that be my goal in life.
Say I am but a simple man.

No Fences and an Axe

The man next door leaves his axe out in the rain.
We are not neighbors, in the sense
Of fences and good neighbors. I don't
Know his name; for two years we have waved
And said something mundane about the weather
As we passed. He's skinny and gray and looks
Like a salted redneck; he drives his golf cart
Up and down the road. I look like a guy
Who walks his dog up and down the same road.
Sometimes people ask if I know *so and so* who lives
On Maple Street, Oak or Pine, and I say no.
I think maybe I should, then I think
Of my grandmother who when befuddled
Said to grandkids *you, you. You know
Who you are.* I want to pick up
His axe and move it out of the rain, set
It on his porch, but who am I and who
Is he that I should step on his porch uninvited?

Names of Water

Flood, pond, puddle, lake, tarn,
Biblical rain, meteorologically
speaking, and now I'm sitting
surrounded by the risen waters.
They glitter in the sun like a thousand
diamond rings; pine and palmetto
bounce on the tannin mirror.
Little frogs have found it now,
a twig to sit on, plop from, ripple
the near deep. How many days until
these waters go wherever they go—
into the sand-soaked earth, back
to air. What's the word for walking
on water and naming it home?

Wish You Were Here

We walk out of the East
like wisemen, head west
where Dog Island trolls

the horizon. We walk the same
shore every day: from the sandbar
at Morrison Beach to the derelict

dock. This morning
in the parking lot, cast netters
unload their trucks.

Red Ford, white
Chevy, wet with the
night's rain.

Tropical Storm Eta, Alligator Point

We stand here on the shore,
two old men and a dog. His cast net
in a paint bucket. Tide lapping our feet.

He says he'd hoped waves would lay down.
Neither of us mentions the new storm,
Greek because we've run out of letters, gathering

its second wind, turning north toward us.
No glass minnows, greenies, pinfish.
His bucket empty.

Requiem for a Junked Mullet Smoker

The trash picker passes it by. Time
isn't kind, no match for neglect.
Rust and decay, ineluctable metaphors
once we get old enough to believe
we aren't immortal. Some learn
this early, some too late.
It's easier for a smoker to get to heaven
than an old man to pass through eye
of a camel, or a needle. You say,
I can buy mullet in Panacea for a few bucks.
No fucking with fire, lighting coals,
watching them go out. No forgetting
to grease the grill so that skin
doesn't stick. Oh, such little and many
complaints. That's life too.
The fog is thick over the State Park
like it's coming out of the sand
pines, stepping softly like a bobcat,
like the coyotes that howl in the evenings
when the sun falls again and again.

Just Past Dawn We Walk to the Beach

                    Soon
I will not be able to open
the bear-proof trash can. Fingers
too weak, the awkward, backward
twist of arm it takes to lift the heavy steel
lid, too much.

Below the dunes, six dolphins
rise to breathe, swim
toward the rising sun.

Is this enough found to balance lost?

Throwing Starfish Back into the Sea

They sprawl as if fallen from the sky.
I'm told all of them are not dead.
The ones not bone-dry, ones without severed
limbs, might live if returned to the water.
I'm told too that they can inch their way
to the shore break. Though I have time
to wish and watch, I lack patience. After
my friend leaves I pick one up and fling
it like a frisbee toward the surf.
Another, three, four, five. I wonder
if the dolphins feeding near shore
eat starfish. I wonder how much
                good I have done.

Hard Rain

Today the rain came like a man.
Its gray camps besieged our sky
on three fronts, backing us

against the Gulf. The first wind
rattled palmetto; the first thunder
rolled across the scrub palms.

Second gust bent pines and buckled
the roof of our trailer. Thunder
broke again, closer, shook frail windows.

Rain strafed sheet metal walls.
We hid. My old dog under
a too-small table and a closet full of shoes.

This too shall pass, I whispered, but
hummed *wasn't that a mighty storm
that blew all the people away.*

Walking Meditation

On the shell road a green snake
dies more every day, flattens
and sinks into sand. Light
dances off the harbor. Water
oaks twist like sisters bent
in the wind. Believe me.
Believe that I believe in something
hard to name. Finger mullet
schooling near dock pilings.
Mangrove roots snagging my feet.
The sky over brown oyster bars.
Morning grass, still wet and cold, gleaming
like tongues of a thousand little gods.

THE LIGHT WE CALL WINTER

If you see me walking down
the shell road under myrtle

and Spanish moss, don't worry.
The road's a circle and it brings me

back to my yellow mailbox.
You might give me the name

of the bird that sat all morning
on the thin branch.

Give me the last lost months gone
in a haze, sloughed off like an old dog

shakes himself dry.
Walk with me.

I won't say
I don't need you.

Fish Streets before Dawn

Sometimes we drive down
past the fish streets to see
if everything is still there.
Kingfish, trout, grouper,
cobia. Even the sleeping beach
houses, softly lit, look like
they belong here. On my right
the Gulf sky does its rosy dawn
thing. Left, dark pines
and oak hammocks spot
the tall grasses. At the end
of the road I turn back.
Each moment the sky lightens.

Two Lane Highway to Panacea

Where the road cuts the marsh,
    tide rising over oyster bars
        and through winter brown reeds

I'm complaining about the old man
    in a blue pickup
        doing 45 in a 45

I swing out to pass, grumbling
    "old people" and see him
        ramrod straight, hands at ten

and two, John Deere cap
    above his glasses. Where
        do I have to hurry to?

Where do I need to be?
    The Dollar General, post office,
        the Crawfordville drug store?

Once I had a sleek rental car cranked
    up to 80 on the highway outside
        of Tallahassee

when the Highway Patrol
    pulled me over and asked
        "What's your need for speed?"

I didn't know, but tried to engage him in the spirit
    of James Dean, Brando, and other philosophers
        I only half understood:

"Speed has its own need." He wrote me a ticket.
    25 over the limit.
        Not for this old man.

OTHER PLACES

Touching the Heart Means a Steal of Home

I am a back-up catcher, Single A,
Big Sky League. I've found my calling.
Nothing to write home about, but
I do it twice a week to a woman
I loved, but not enough. I told her
I had to follow my heart; she didn't
understand why it had to lead me away
from her. Last week she wrote
when you're done warming up pitchers
in a bare dirt bullpen, remember what
you've lost. It was a sign. The sky's large
enough for all of us to get lost. Nighthawks
dive for bugs in stadium lights never bright
enough. When I go home it will be too late.

Pittsburgh Ritual

Packed into the Buick, every remembered year
we drive through downtown Pittsburgh—
Fifth Ave and Forbes, Smithfield and Penn.
Christmas lights, storefront displays
of Gimbels and Horne's. For fifteen minutes
the night is radiant, streetlights, red lights,
headlights sparkle and split into diamonds
across our windshield. A trolley clatters
past, white shards from its electric
wire tinsel the cold sky. We drive
slowly, but don't stop. We come
to look not shop. When time is up
we cross the Allegheny to the dark
Northside, down Route 65
past the mills, the Legion, home.

Another Story of Ash

I am carrying my brother,
bone, skin, hair, teeth, nails
in a box. Our dead call for ritual,
but since we had given up on a god,
I brought him home to the Little League field
and scattered some of him in the outfield
grass. The first rain will wash him away,
but I'll remember years of summer days here
where locust trees crowded the right field fence.

The soot and ash days are gone.
My brother knew this game better
than he played it; he's left the life
he screwed up. I remain,
lucky. No good reason to outlive
a hard fastball, and everything
this broken life threw at us.

In Late Recognition of Prince

On the shoulder of the highway
past Rochester, Minnesota,
I found a raspberry beret. I
wasn't a fan. I was in my first
stage of calcification—old
before I'd grow older. I
didn't need another hot guitar
player. I had Hendrix, Duane,
and Stevie Ray. Clapton was still alive.
So the beret, dull with road dust,
crusted with grime, I left where
it lay. What did I know of what
was to come, how much of everything
I could know stretched across the brown
swale in a field turning to green.

Thinking of Frost and the Calabrian Miners Dead in West Virginia

12/7/1907

Three roads diverged in a green wood.
They were worn much differently for different purpose.
Mahogany Road rutted, weeds deep where it curved out of sight.
Mine Road 63 rising gravel gray into sumac and beech.
The river trail passed through dappled sunlight

to disappear in green dark canopy. I knew
as way led away from way that I was unlikely to walk
the road to the Monongah Mine's dead. I supposed too,
that in days hence I would write and maybe sigh:
I took the road I always take; has it made any difference?

The Old Places

for Philip Levine

Here, in the modern invention
of South Florida, I am trying
to remember a place that never was.
The ever and never changing malls,
gated communities with names
that conjure the idyllic out of palmetto
and scrub. I point to a road heading
west to more real estate and say
that's mine. I flagged its only curve
and measured half mile sections
to the horizon. On the rich
island's forbidden green
streets I take two quiet steps
on paver blocks I laid and tamped
with my German foreman and redneck crew.
All over this county there's roads I drove
trucks down, condo stairs I carried sofas
and washing machines up. Out
on Haverhill when it was the western edge
of all that had been bought and sold, I
pounded on an ex-girlfriend's door
at 3 a.m. and then slept off a mushroom
trip in the back seat of her unlocked
VW. I used to call the Singer Island
shoreline, where every high tide
washed away the evidence
that I was ever here, home.

What I Might Know about Indiana

for Michael Martone

Elwood, where my mother was born
and her father bought three houses
in the Thirties for next to nothing
then gave two to poor neighbors. Anderson
where I hitchhiked to see a great Aunt
who had never seen me, and after
I convinced her I was Rosemary's son
she wept, took me to meet a street
of second cousins. Gary, where
Uncle Frank, sleeve folded
over a ghost arm lost in a factory
stood in a dark doorway.

This Train is Not Going to NY

It's not going to Florida either,
to the peninsula that hooks
into the Gulf, the shank
of which I live on. This is not
the train for NY. By tonight
I will drive down shell roads,
what moon is up shining over
scrub pine and palmetto
across my backyard fence.

A thousand miles south of NY
my dog and I will climb stairs
to the front door and fumble
the key into the lock. I will
be happy to not be in NY.
Someday, when I am younger
some other train might take me
there and I'll eat oysters in Grand
Central or look again for the avenue
that bears the initial of Christ
into the new and aging world.

On Each Bead We Said Three Hail Marys

On a long straight highway in middle
Georgia, I realized I did not believe
in God. Nothing from those Catholic

days still worked but my Irish grandma
Lucy's advice to keep my feet clean
in case I went to the hospital.

After I rolled my Fairlane
into the mangroves on Singer Island
I went to the ER with swamp mud feet.

Keep all twenty mysteries on hand.

The Sorrowful Mystery was my mother's,
divorced, forbidden her sacrament.
There's no longer a Luminous Mystery. God's

a long time gone. Alone in the dark
when wind ripples the trailer roof
I ask for her mercy. Glory Be.

With James Wright as My Spiritual Guide, I Drive through Southeast Ohio Looking for Ancestors

Nothing. The clerk in the Salineville
Sunoco knew nothing about our name.
No one in my family mattered
much. Our obituaries are short.
No record of where we were

before here. No crossing, no settling.
No old country. Scotland and Ireland
spit us out with no return address.

On a hilltop graveyard, headstones
of salt miners, farmers, mothers, daughters,
none of them mine, ringed

a marker for The Battle of Salineville,
small by all standards except to the few
who died in the valley below. Maybe

my Campbells were among the anonymous
militia troops fighting a forgotten moment.
Preparing to be unknown forever.

Sometimes the Song Tells You Who You Are

I lived all my life somewhere below Lake Marie.
Most of everything I know is there. Pittsburgh,
the Ohio, flood canals out of Okeechobee. I've
watched moccasins glide past the tea green eyes

of alligators and covered my face with a bandana
as the Pahokee cane fields burned. I know Lake Marie,
the lost daughter, like it was home and home
was always hard to find. That two-bit tract house

on a hill above the tracks, apartments and trailers
in South Florida. One place after another full of roaches
they called college life. What's left of my hometown
shrink wrapped in a box, mailed and lost.

The radio playing *Oh Baby,*
We Gotta Go Now

XENOGLOSSY

I once wrote of my mill town
that you can *want* all your life here.
I was in love with words and
the directions they might lead:
into the temple of furnace fire
and out again? Along
a ridge with hawks drafting
thermals? Blues as it's bent
at the crossroads? Freight trains
clacking downriver under the cloaked moon?
Just empty space?

At night I speak in the tongues
of angels and fools: babble
imperfect definitions of desiderate, lack,
                              ought.

Yesterday, blades of grass parted
as the pygmy rattler sidled away
from my boot. I wanted to call
the hawk in the pine tree
down to snatch it up, but
I had no tongue for hawk.

What did I know? I am older.
It wasn't just home that wanted,
not just the valley that lacked.

Derecho

I had a girlfriend from Cedar Rapids who had a streak of pink hair. We lived on the high plains where trees were mostly cotton woods along the rivers, and those that people planted to ring houses and line streets. Her Cedar Rapids trees are gone now. We lived in a basement apartment and never saw a tree through our little windows. The campus and the city watered trees from ground level aqueducts. I had come there from a land of so much rain that the quaint irrigation system made me smile. Home was streets full of water, puddles big as buses. I imagine her looking at a million broken and ravaged trees. She used to say *fucking weird* a lot. So much struck her that way, me included. Her pink swatch would shake left and right, curls falling across her face. In Wyoming trees were scarce as people. The wind blew all the time.

December, Big Sur

Butterflies in the brown grass
of the swale look for the sun.
Cold is not their best of all worlds.

It is late in their lives. They
are almost still as wildflowers. I
walk miles of road waiting for a ride,

the ocean blue and breaking
below the sky. I pick one up,
monarch, maybe, I'm never sure.

Fooled by mimicry like birds.
I think of Eberhart's wasps, how
he warmed them to near flying

then cooled them again. This one,
will it warm in my hands and fly,
grateful for my gift?

It twitches, then the wind
blows it away.
It's easy to forget.

Telluride, Abandoned Mine Shaft

On this bright mountain, bleached timbers,
rusted mine carts, rubble
down the scree slope

to a thin creek. From
the shaft, rail tracks twist
like stunned promises.

Slow havoc
was wreaked here.
The milk of home.

Wyoming Ranch Road

We stopped for permission to cross.
How much is yours, I asked.
How much can you see? That morning
from the Front Range to Medicine Bow,
miles of high prairie, a dark line
of cottonwoods watered
by the North Platte. We drove west,
climbed switchbacks, washboarded
across Battle Pass. The sun fell red
on Bridger Mountain.

Tucumcari

I was never a hippy. Didn't believe
in stars and karma. Aquarius was a pop
song that couldn't hang with Whippin' Post.
I knew how to work forty hours a week
but often chose not to. Love was never free.
I hitched from Barstow through Tucumcari
and no girl in a flatbed Ford ever slowed
to look at me. Still, it was a life as fine as one
lives without money or flashback embellishments.
Four days cross country, good rides.
No one killed me.

Practicing Silence

Outside of NYC, it's
almost impossible
to be mistaken

for a mime. Here,
at the edge of the country
I'm just a guy who moves

silently down crushed shell
roads, through pine forests
in deep sand, past the harbor's

broken docks. Ok, yes,
I could talk more, but to whom,
the clerk at the Dollar General?

What would I find worth saying
more than thanks? Buzzards whirl
over my head like synchronized swimmers.

What's Been Lost

Love Is Not a Victory March

It's come to this. Freezing
night. A quarter moon in the sky,
one star, bright as a spaceship
hovering in the South, somewhere
over the water. Too cold to sing,
we walk, particulates of dust and pollen
float in my headlamp beam.
Florescent bugs glow like jewels
in the grass. Love, how far away it is,
dark and round at the edge of a lake's
satellite image, with what could be trees
ringing the shore from heart to heart
as the crow flies. Who
can fly with crows, love?

On Dying Too Soon after Finally Finding Love

for James Wright

When your love lights the trees
of your East River Park, shouldn't you
get another lifetime? That's not
just a rhetorical question.

It's cold this morning. Walking the dog,
fingers brittle, the trash truck beeps
two shell roads over. As he squats, I watch
a white squirrel chase a gray from pine
to pine. The gray scrambles up the trunk
then reverses, like a runner in the open field,
or a soldier dodging enemy fire, and leaps
across to the tree he just left. The white
remains still, content, I guess, to claim
his tree. About love. About age.
About death. What do squirrels know?

Don't Burn Again for Nothing

after Gerald Stern

I would make you a promise
that the world will turn
toward good, but you're no fool
to the way worlds turn, and you
know my powers and promises
often fall short. Don't burn, love.
There's a small grove of wax myrtle
and cedar. Its shade is honey
when the sun is high and hot.
Bees gather there to rest.
If you burn, I'll try to soothe you
with aloe and oils. I will bring you
grapes, peaches, and cakes.
What's this all about, you ask.
I don't know. I don't know.

Shoes and Shirts Last Longer than a Man

Bones and teeth last longer too,
but likes shoes and shirts they were never
a man, just synecdoche, parts standing

for the whole, but not as well
as a good hand on the ranch,
a good eye at the plate. A good poet

sings *I knew a woman lovely in her bones.*
There are few odes about teeth.
Last night I read about homeless men

stripping dead bodies for warm shirts,
for better boots; clothes living on,
but not a man, not his bones.

The Angel of Winter Won't Remember Your Name

Oh, angels. The best of them petulant,
grousing about having to watch over
His new inferior, ungainly pets

prone to so much human error.
The worst, we know: Lucifer
& his failed fallen followers, tumbling

nine days from the cliffs of heaven
to the steaming shores of hell. God
always seems to have a plan. A hell

for demons, Eden to be lost, resurrection
waiting. Forgiveness. Oh forgiveness.

The Rapture Coming

The world ends every day. By day
we mean an arbitrary line running
through the Chatham Islands where the last
minute ends and the first begins. A time
between now and then, or when you
turn your back on a loved one. By end
we mean change. The world is not
what it was before the car crash,
before surgery, before your dog died.
Not what it was before you fell in love
and clearly not what it was after your lover
left. The world ends today, again.
Wings beating the air.

EDEN

> *We entered the house. We loved*
> *everyone. Our hearts were bursting.*
> —Frank X. Gaspar

Then only I knew how *the full Eden*
of it—a sort of a priori entrapment,
like buying Indian ponies or grass
from a narc—is easily lost.

Now there's this: he claimed
it was about truth and beauty. Truth
leaves us stranded. The old persimmon
rotted, cracked near the ground
and fell fully green and leaved.
Beauty's an idea, it does not need us
to fulfill its being.

All of this—Truth, Beauty, Eden,
I suspect, is not enough.

All those words / around our glowing heads.
Isn't that what we make that world with?

Maybe, I say now, maybe.
We all end up mourned, forgotten,
each in its turn. Now, yes, I've gone
too far: what's left is desire.
I'm tired. The heart's a wheel, bent
but carrying me down the road.

Pawning His Guitar

In grad school he'd pawn his guitar
almost every month and get it back
when the stipend came. The pawnbroker
liked him and took good care of his axe. Now
he has a room full of guitars—Martin, Gibson,
Telecaster, Gretsch. He'd admit
he earned these by being lucky
and unlucky in love, gotten so much
he could be blessed, lost so much nothing
he has really matters. He plays
from a notebook of scribbled songs. I ask
what key we're in and he doesn't know.
Capoed down three frets, we do a math problem,
then give up. He plays. I listen.
I play. We look at each other and nod.

What's Emptiness Got to Do with It?

I'm pondering glimmering nature
as it drifts over
the weedy forgotten lot,

walking down the shell road,
light fading, looking at the vulture tree,
empty all winter like sullen

market stalls: no peaches,
honey, soap, and spices. Angels
too, gone, singing *Jolene, Jolene.*

JOHN PRINE'S BAND

In the last few months
I've watched these men
I don't know grow old
like family. They've gone
gray in my living room, some
nights aging twenty years
as the café empties and the lights
go dark. This is how we live
an elegy, how the funeral train
rolls slowly through town: far
from us and yet always here,
a song we've sung since songs began.

Instant Replay

The play is over, but it's not.
Somewhere in NY or heaven
some guys are reviewing
our effort to make something
of ourselves, to be a good father,
to do the right thing. We've come close
of course, that's why our life's under
review. They watch us fall again
and again. In one frame we make the line
to gain, in another, come up short.

The play-by-play man says what we always feel:
if only we could see this from another angle.
Something's always in the way. Children, work, love,
lack of love, a crappy father, bad luck,
weak will, empty soul. Inconclusive evidence,
they say, after we've looked, searched, played it
over and over again. You never know
where your knee hit the turf.

JUMPING THE VW BUS

It works like this: take it out of gear.
Turn the key on. Get your screwdriver
from under the seat. Walk back
to the right rear tire. Are you sure
it's out of gear? Reach up, lay the blade
across the solenoid terminals. Having
little faith in prayer, start rolling from under
the bus. Let your breath out as the damn
thing starts and does not crush your skull.
Smile if someone is watching. Be cool
as you dust the sand off your arms and legs.
Climb back into the front seat. Don't
stall the car when you shift into first.

Figurative Language

Like this guy Jan, my party
chief, told us when we were waiting
out a Florida rain—truck windows
steamed, humidity and maybe
pot too. He says *no shit man.*
We were flying in this thick soup
and I'm looking everywhere
for the carrier deck. I got my face
pressed to the cockpit glass. I'm
saying I don't see it man and the pilot's
starting to freak. I look up to my right
and there it is. Like a cliff with dim lights
and I say, shit, shit, pull up man. We're
like ten feet above the waves.

2.

I live alone. AC only cools one room.
I hang feathers before the vent
so that I can watch them float.
My dog, half a big as I am, sprawls
sideways across the bed, I don't bother
to move him. I thought there
would be more and once there was.

3.

There's this too: the hawk on the mailbox
staring as we walk the cracked cement
driveway. The bananas in the yard a few
houses down that finally ripened.
The blue tarp on the roof because a loblolly
fell during the last hurricane. A lizard
that runs up the brick wall as I close the door.
The many places my dog relieves himself
on the high bank above Tharpe Street.
Lights in all the houses we walk by
though no one lives in some of them.

Poem for the Day John Prine Died

I don't think I ever prayed
without being forced to. Ten
Hail Marys, three Our Fathers,

an Act of Contrition. I confessed
some made-up sins, embellished
my venial faults to seem

worthy. Then I quit.
God wasn't doing me any favors.
South Florida was so far from the Celestial

Palace that even my sad mother
couldn't hear the angels sing. The God
who made me floated above smoke

stacks, his fingers stained with soot.
But today, sun rising over the Gulf,
                Dear Lord

Hide & Seek

Sandy B and I hid in garages.
We were never found until we wanted
to be. I was twelve and she
two years older—a woman
of the world. Blond, leggy, Twiggy thin.
She'd tell me what junior high would be like
next year. I wanted her to kiss me
because I had never been kissed.
She was beautiful. The one, the one
because she was the only girl
in the game. She had a transistor
tuned to WAMO. We listened to Porky
Chedwick, the *Daddio of the Raddio*, spin
soul grooves from upriver in Pittsburgh.
"Under the Boardwalk," "Come See About Me."
"Quicksand." "Baby Love." We leaned
against Mr. K's green Bel Air, touching hips,
not touching anything else.

Five Miles from Wherever I Am

The post office says I live
in Panacea and while that's good
enough to cure most ills

it won't be mistaken for Paradise.
Sometimes it easy to forget
that Paradise was forsaken, down

by the Green River and wherever
Milton's was too. The coal company
took one; we gave the other away.

There's no end of shovels
coming for those
always too late in asking.

Unfriending the Writer More Famous Than I

My life is a museum. I am cranky.
My kitchen is tormented, gods
bouncing off the walls, lost
voices crying look for tomorrow.
A small hawk, Kestrel maybe,
sat on the wire as we walked
to the beach & I knew
I'd come back with a bag of shit
in my pocket. Life's not always
dark, not just mucking out the stables
of someone's mess. Some short number
of years ago we actually had to know
someone before saying
you're no longer my friend. You
were a name on the spine of a book
and one of us accepted the other.
You might be a better person than I.
You might carry dog shit in a thin
plastic bag too. I will never know.

The Gun

I shot a pistol once at a can
and missed. Now, my knowledge
enhanced by crime novels and TV,
I think it might have been a .45
because it was long. Not an automatic
with a clip, not a Glock or a Sig, firing
ten shots quicker than I could breathe.

When I was a kid I might have hit
a bird with a rock, but it might also
have been Chuckie, the slow kid.
I remember both of us, open-mouthed disbelief
that it had been hit, then a small horror
as it fell. My litany of death is longer now.
Snakes. A raccoon the dogs had maimed,
and maybe my brother who I could not save
                      from himself.

I held a gun one more time. Stuck
in a minor drug deal, a guy said here
hold this in case some shit goes down. Yes,
it had a B-movie script. Nothing
went down and I walked
away—whole, light, glowing.

Dream of Nowhere Home

I was walking down Phillips Street's long hill
& where it dove into State Street,
where I used to fear the car wouldn't
stop, or might tumble roof over wheels
into the beauty salon, there was a mall
of chrome & glass. Boutiques & beautiful
young women behind large windows. Gone
the old brick drugstore, grocery & dairy.
I walked through the mall & thought
of my grandparent's flat above the donut
shop. None of the glassed shops were open.
The concourse rose up hill.
There seemed no way out until a fire
escape door loomed on the right. I
went down three flights & walked
out into a street I did not know.
The Methodist Church & the Riverview
Hotel with the widow's walk where
barge captains used to stay, were gone.
I walked upriver toward Pittsburgh
but suspected it too was no longer there.

Rick Campbell is a poet and essayist living on Alligator Point, Florida. His most recent book is a collection of essays, *Sometimes the Light* (Main Street Rag Press). Poetry collections include: *Provenance* (Blue Horse Press); *Gunshot, Peacock, Dog* (Madville Publishing); *The History of Steel* (All Nations Press); *Dixmont* (Autumn House Press); *Setting the World in Order* (Texas Tech University Press); *The Traveler's Companion* (Black Bay Books); and *A Day's Work* (State Street Press). His poems and essays have appeared in many journals and anthologies, including *The Georgia Review*, *Fourth River*, *Kestrel*, *Alabama Literary Review*, and *Prairie Schooner*. He's won a Pushcart Prize and an NEA Fellowship in Poetry. He teaches in the University of Nevada-Reno's MFA program.

Printed in the USA
CPSIA information can be obtained
at www.ICGtesting.com
LVHW092239230224
772664LV00003B/375